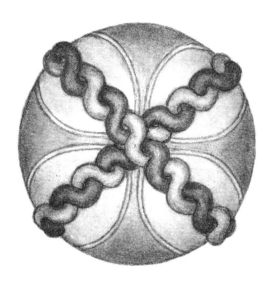

Published by:
Foundation House Publications
P.O. Box 9, 100 Mile House, B.C.
Canada V0K 2E0
(604) 395-2485

In the United States
4817 North County Road 29
Loveland, Colorado 80537
U.S.A. (303) 679-4300

First Printing March 1988
Second Printing May 1988
Third Printing November 1988
Fourth Printing May 1990
Fifth Printing April 1992

MAGIC
AT OUR HAND

Releasing Our Lives into Order and Beauty

NANCY ROSE EXETER

DRAWINGS BY THE AUTHOR

Acknowledgments

I acknowledge the many wonderful people who have contributed richly to my own life and learning, and who assisted in myriad ways in bringing forth this book.

My special thanks to Janice Wheeler for her artistic hand in cover design and layout, and to Judith Smookler for her months of perceptive editorial assistance.

Nancy Rose Exeter

Contents

Poetry

Like a shaft of light piercing still, dark waters, *Magic at our Hand* illuminates the recesses of our deepest selves. With her insights, her poetry and her drawings, Nancy Rose Exeter invites you to share in her experience of the sacred in living. Drink freely of her inspiration, the silent currents of upliftment and renewal released in her words. Let them penetrate where they may, for your own magic will answer.

The Editors

1.

Opening Doors

I greet you. We are together on this earth, and even if we have never met, there is a potent magic that can connect us. We as human beings share invisible currents of thought and feeling more than we may notice in our daily rounds. As you open this book, your world and my world, you and I, have a point of connection. I welcome that, and am somehow assured that we will recognize each other in this invisible meeting.

There is so much more to us, to each human being, than the physical and obvious. Who has not had a sense that he or she was in essence much greater, stronger and more beautiful than the personality that appears to others in the everyday world? Is this sensing just a fantasy, or is it a deeper self knocking at the doors of consciousness?

We have all experienced moments where events worked together in a marvelous and elegant way, where our part in them was handled lightly and well, and there was a feeling of power moving through us without our having to have power *over* anyone or anything. Because these experiences are seen through our usual habits of thinking, we may not notice the elements that were at play in allowing this magic to work.

The word "magic" usually has the connotation of sleight of hand, that which seems to be so but is only a trick. That kind of deceptive magic may be entertaining, or confusing, but is just a manipulation in the surface play of things. The magic of which I speak moves in us and surrounds us. It is that which may not seem, but is.

Everywhere in the natural world are evidences of design, of a remarkable intelligence that fits everything together—from the migration of birds to the function of individual cells in a living body. The design of our own being is equally remarkable and includes dimensions which, in the usual course of events, we touch and experience only occasionally, and seemingly by chance. We may discount those private experiences of

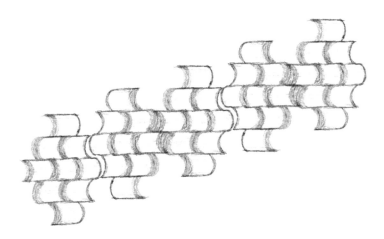

beauty, vision or well-being because there is no
apparent outer reason for them, but it is impossible to experience anything that is not in some
way part of us. In those transcendent moments
we must have opened a door that is always
present and available.

There is a yearning in the human soul for
larger meaning, depth, and vividness of experience, for full-spectrum expression of self, for genuine communion and accomplishment in relationships with others. The sense that these longings
are not fruitless and unrealistic, but are telling us
what is possible and even natural, is beginning to
stir in many people. Magic of this kind is our
birthright, and we need only discover how to

align with its working. Magic is at hand, both around us and through us.

My brother Lloyd Meeker speaks of this in his poem, "The Return of Magic":

Rest with me and remember again
The passage of magic from our realm
Long ago, banished by barbarians.
Grieve for our ages in an empty world
Of brittle sky and hard thin earth;
We should but weep and turn again away
Had we not just seen glimmer
The olden glow's grainy lustre
Flicker soft where one passed walking—
And had seen others seeing.

It is enough—for magic has returned.
Secretly we smile, knowing,
And with one breath
Wash away our empty interlude
Full only of imitation,
And rest in light together
Far from cold mid-winter memories
Of circled figures on barren moors
Waiting for the sun.
It is enough—for magic has returned.

This ever-present dimension is either received, or excluded, in our own consciousness. It is we, humankind, who have excluded magic by our hard-heartedness and self-determinations. Magical potentials are again manifesting in the world as there are human beings willing and able to accommodate them. It is for us to discover how to give admittance to this heritage of beauty and power, how to open ourselves to our deepest Truth.

We discover that there is a magic in being,

that our very presence is significant.

2.

The Still Place

Much of what we do can be seen as motivated by a desire for peace of mind. We may go to quiet wilderness settings or amass substantial bank accounts, but it is our individual capacity to *experience* peace and stillness that is at question. The real urge is to be inwardly at peace, in equilibrium.

What process must we move through to come to this? In the final analysis this brings each one of us to the nub of our very sense of being, our sense of purpose. There is no way to come fully to rest without coming to terms with the elemental questions of: What is my purpose in being on earth? What am I doing here? The way our lives manifest may seem to have little to do with that deeper sense of ourselves. What are we to do to bring the potential we feel into the light of day?

We are, by nature, creators. We actively create what is contained in our lives. Although we often seem to be pressured in one direction or another, we are making choices constantly, and the cumulative effect of them is either clutter and confusion, or peace. I think everybody would prefer to have emotional stability, a foundational equilibrium, as the basis for handling the vicissitudes brought to us in the course of our days. But as we well know, wishing for stability doesn't produce it; trying for it doesn't work. Determination not to be pushed around does not produce peace but rather a hardness of heart and the frustration of bottling up one's feelings, which in the end is only destructive.

Our lives are full of pushes and pulls. We feel we have responsibilities we must carry; there is no way around them. We have had experiences through our growing-up years which have left their scars, and there are sore places that tend to get hit by things that come along. All of this seems so inevitable. The urge to try to escape, in whatever way, arises out of the conviction that all these influences control us. But we are only controlled if we allow it, if we allow ourselves to be immersed in what goes on around us. We can choose to be in a different place in our own consciousness.

Human experience can be described in terms of a series of concentric rings. If we picture our very self as the point at the center, the rings further out from that point may represent various levels of experience: feelings, sensings, thoughts and observations, events. Most of us tend to think of ourselves as existing amidst these rings rather than at the center point. But if our sense of self is out among all the things that we have to take care of, the things that are desirable or that hurt, the forces that impinge, there seems no way to be stable, to come to rest. What is the process by which we may move progressively back from all of this that goes on, so we may come finally into the center place where we are at rest and where our perspective is a clear and balanced one?

This center place relates to a sense of purpose. It has to do with the experience of who we are in a unique sense, who each of us is, and what it is that we, I, can bring, can let emerge through myself that is unique, different from any other being.

All of the decisions that have to be made about career, partner, children, other milestones in life, are usually made because of factors in the outer rings. But the central consideration really is: What is it that I can *bring* to whatever it is I choose to do?

There is a flow that emerges from each being, either impeded or free. If our identity and attachments are out in the rings, then the flow

which emerges from the center point is hindered;
it can't get through all of the things that are in
the way. It's only as we move back in consciousness, in awareness, and abide in the still
point at the center, where we actually belong,
that the experience of this flow becomes full and
meaningful. Probably we have all experienced
this at different times and in different degrees,
but the issue is how to stay there consciously and
consistently.

Our lives are so cluttered with combinations
of priorities that we need to take some quiet time
to bring them into perspective. What is the
greatest priority? When it gets right down to it, if
I don't bring forth what is uniquely mine to
bring, then there will not have been much point
in my having been here on earth. There is really
nothing more important than being in place, in
that place of equilibrium from which a current
may move and do whatever it should in a
situation.

In facing this, we see the need to let go of the things that hold us away from that center point. What keeps us bound are our habitual ways of handling things: our self-defenses, our desires, our opinions about how everything should work. But we can't really let go of these emotional elements that hold us in the wrong positioning until we realize what we can let go *to*. It's impossible, because all these defenses and structures were developed for self-preservation. Until we realize that we don't need to preserve ourselves, that we will be safe without defenses, we can't bring ourselves to let go of them. But we can and must let go to the way things really work, because ultimately they are going to work that way anyway. We have to acknowledge that the way we as a race have tried to make things work has not produced what we intended. We are at a very dangerous juncture, and the destiny of the whole world is in question.

To be able to let go enough to perceive what *is* working and let that come into our immediate situations is the great skill needed. There is an emanation from every aspect of life—animals, plants, the earth itself—and it all harmonizes; it is all part of one great flow. The mere fact of the consistency of the day and night, the steadiness of the seasons, we take for granted. But when you think of what a precarious balance this little earth is in, what a slight change in our distance from the sun would do to the planet and all its life-forms, you realize that there is something to be trusted. Something has kept us in this delicately balanced orbit. Something keeps fine-tuning all the immensely intricate elements in what we call ecology.

Oneness, harmony, is natural. What comes forth through me—if it is true, if it is factually the expression of my self from the center point—is a harmonious and useful part of the overall flow, the overall rhythm. As we let go in any specific situation to whatever is true, whatever is right, so that the current can move, we inevitably find that we are safe in doing that; we are not actually vulnerable. We are far safer in that center position than we were when we were relying on all our self-created structures, which can be knocked down with every wind that blows.

The ability to live in the still point springs from a respect for being, for what flows out of being, for one's own simple presence. We have tended to assume that everything happens in the outer rings, in what shows, where results are visible. We discover that there is a magic in being, that our very presence is significant. It is not just what we say or do. It is often in our silences that something can be offered that is true and valuable, that is a blessing. Out of Being flows the magic of manifold creation—all the color, the excitement, the nuance and beauty, that can be part of human experience.

Winter Solstice

The year gathers,
laden,
into stillness:
a heartbeat in the warmth
of internal dark.
A long, ardent embrace,
a smiling inhalation

and the year steps out on the crisp
glint of dawn,
exhaling a bright spring wind.

The choices are made subtly,
but what we let ourselves get away with
determines what our world turns out to be.

3.

The Real Choices

One of the assumptions that virtually everyone makes is that life consists of making conscious decisions. In whatever cultural terms, in whatever type of situation, this is the assumption: that we can consciously determine what should happen and then make it happen. (And if we can't, it's because of terrible injustices!) A rather high compliment that can be paid to almost anybody nowadays is that they are decisive—they know what they want and they go after it.

Yet when we try to create a specific effect because of a decision about what should occur, it never seems to work out just the way we think it will. It's like the devil giving you three wishes. It doesn't matter what you wish for, some twist is going to come in. In my observation, there is no way we can *decide* what should happen. There are always variables that we can't anticipate, and if we have a hard and fast agenda of any kind, no matter how praiseworthy, something is going to go awry.

And that's how we find the state of the world today—awry. Surely the intentions of almost everyone are good, at least for themselves and their families. Yet with all these good intentions, if we look at any field—the economy, the environment, international relations—we see increasing problems.

In trying to make a decision we never have all the factors at our disposal, and that's why decisions often go wrong. It's usually just the surface factors that we can grasp mentally. We can make a column of pros and a column of cons, but that's not enough. If we are going to make a right choice, what we are sensing and what we are absorbing as information must be more than just the surface play, just the pros and cons. We have to include invisible factors that we may perceive but probably can't articulate. Because we listen for these invisible indicators of how our actions fit into a larger tapestry, we begin to develop a sense of how to stay in balance, how to act wisely.

Decisions made merely at the mental level

cannot work. This seems a heretical thing to say, especially in our sophisticated civilization where there is so much focus on learning, on education, so that we can "make the right decisions." Author Laurens van der Post has said: "One of the great problems of our time is that we know too much for our own good. Our knowledge, instead of increasing our sense of responsibility, has been corrupted by the power it has conferred."

Though some education can be valuable, the right directions are determined at a different level of experience, a place where there is resonance with a great overall sense of creation. There is something larger which constantly seems to thwart the surface decisions we try to make anyway, so it seems the better part of wisdom to acknowledge that we exist in this larger context and act appropriately within it.

How then do we rightly exercise our ability to choose? We do, in fact, make choices constantly as to what we will entertain in our thoughts and

feelings—whether we will let an unpleasant incident, for instance, go round and round, while we formulate comebacks like "I should have..." and "Next time I see him I'm going to..." We may be doing it unthinkingly, but nevertheless we are making a choice, a choice to maintain internal clutter in regard to that person or that event. Then there is a barrier between ourselves and that person next time we see them, which wouldn't have been there otherwise.

Our lives are full of might-have-beens: careers that might have opened up, relationships that might have held steady, friendships that might have been mutually nurturing—so many things that could have been if we hadn't allowed this kind of emotional debris to be harbored and to get in the way. The choices are made subtly, but what we let ourselves get away with determines what our world turns out to be.

The great irony is that we have tended to assume that we can't help how we feel. We presume that how everybody else acts necessarily impinges on us, and we have no choice in our response. And yet where we thought we *had* choice—for example, when we look back at milestones in our lives where we thought we were in control, making decisions this way or that—if we look realistically we can now see that so much happened that we couldn't control at all, that wasn't really our choice, but just happened. Meanwhile, the very place where we have customarily thought we didn't have the ability to choose—our internal state—is the one place where we actually do.

It is such a common habit to mirror the feelings of the people around us. There is a story of two businessmen, one of whom was visiting the other in his hometown. The resident businessman stopped at a newsstand on his way to work, and the man selling newspapers was very surly and spoke rudely to him. The visitor watched in some amazement as his friend cheerily greeted this sour old fellow. After they left the newsstand he said, "How could you be so nice? He was so rude to you." And his friend replied, "Why should I let *him* determine how I behave?"

When we see this, it sounds so simple, it's almost too easy. But it *is* easy! All that is necessary is to maintain this perspective, so that we can develop the internal muscles, the fortitude, to make the right choices. We could call it "quality control between the ears." It is the only place, really, where we have the ability to maintain quality control. This is a profound shift in perspective, because one is assuming the position of being an originator. What we do, our life-action, originates in our own being, and we have the choice as to what will come forth from that point of origination.

There are various dimensions to this realm of inner choice. We have all experienced working away at something and not seeming to get any-

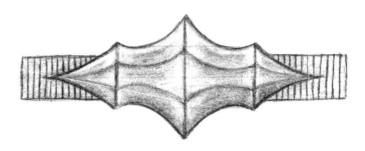

where, and then suddenly, there it is, something gels and the picture is clear. Voluntary work is necessary; we need to open a space by doing carefully whatever work is at hand. The tools we have to do that—the reading, the thinking and conversations, the calculations—all may seem to go nowhere, and yet they open a space that essentially says "yes." The whole mechanism, conscious and subconscious, is working together, whether we are aware of it or not, and suddenly the answer surfaces.

We spend so much time saying "no" because of what we have decided should or shouldn't happen. But quality control between the ears is a space that says, "Yes, let's see what should happen here, let's stay open and do whatever work is at hand to do." The simplicity of heart which just says "yes" to whatever *should* come next makes the space for what rightly can emerge. We might call that experience inspiration, and think of it as rare or maybe reserved for only a few special people. But the experience of inspiration and creativity is a natural one to the human equipment as long as there is space for it to come through.

As we increasingly bring forth in this way, there is a gradual change in our viewpoint and we begin to trust this process. We don't have to try to have faith, or convince ourselves that the right thing will appear, because we have the experience that indeed it will. We begin to feel ourselves on a solid foundation, and there is more and more room to be fully ourselves.

It has been said that most of us die with our music still in us. There is a great deal of music to come forth, but it can only come as we open the way for it. Saying "yes" in these simple ways is also saying "yes" to our participation in the great song of Life. The real choice is to let our music be heard.

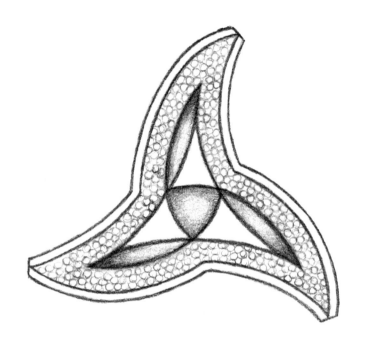

The power that can move through us
    is freed by the power
        of our own internal change.

4.

The Highest Art

Visual art can be a metaphor for the way
we interact, the way we live our lives.
Many wise people have spoken about life as art,
and certainly the ability to live a moment artisti-
cally and beautifully is the highest art there is.
From that all else moves. We may recognize this,
and also take the metaphor a step further.

A piece of art—a lovely object, a painting, a
sculpture—is static, in itself, and yet if this thing
of real beauty is brought into a room and put in
just the right place, something happens. There is
a current generated which is satisfying to anyone
who enters. Something is continually released
and offered by that apparently inactive object.

Spatial relationship—something positioned—is so important in the field of art. A picture placed in just the right position on the wall is satisfying, whereas if it's not in balance with whatever else is in the room, it is not quite right and it doesn't satisfy. This holds true with the color of one object next to another, the line of a sculpture or the theme of a painting.

Such positioning can also apply to our internal spaces, our inner rooms. All of the experiences we have had, or the views that we hold, are either beautiful objects in these inner rooms, in right relatedness to each other, or they are objects that jar—when we look at them something hurts, because we haven't been able to let them take their right position and form.

In our interpersonal relatedness we often try to evoke change in each other, particularly with the ones closest to us. The habit is to prod and to suggest, maybe even to preach a little bit, to hint, maybe to maneuver: "If I do this perhaps he'll do that." We may even shout at times to get our point across: "Damn it, can't you see this?" These attempts to control what is going on in the internal rooms, the house of being, of another person produce only locked doors and pulled-down blinds. No doubt all of us have experienced the sadness of having increased barriers between ourselves and those who matter most in our lives.

When there is awkwardness or confrontation between oneself and another, a change in the "spatial relatedness" can make all the difference. If we are locked in disagreement, both sides refusing to give in, there is an ugly stalemate—no movement, and therefore no means of resolution. But if one person changes attitude, moves a little, then a space is opened up. A change in proximity may be all that is needed—a step back, so that we don't crowd each other, don't defend ourselves, don't assume we know what's being said. This change of line or softening of the form allows the current of feeling to change course.

The word "humility" is another way to describe this movement. The idea of humility doesn't seem to fit with the present fashion of being more assertive—if we were to be humble, we might not receive what we need. But in considering life as art, humility is just a slight shift in positioning, an internal movement—perhaps the release of an opinion, perhaps an affirmation of trust in the larger ecology, knowing that we can safely let go and see what should rightly happen. These shifts in relationship, in quality of presence—a softening, or an opening—can magically change a whole situation. The power that can move through us is freed by the power of our own internal change.

Personal atmosphere is the largest component
of an individual's expression.

5.

A Gentle Breath

I once heard someone say, "If the breeze is warm, people open their windows." While there is a large world for which we are responsible, and we really have very little idea of how far the ripples of our expression extend, the gauge as to whether our individual influence closes windows or opens them involves something very basic in our experience. Simply stated, what kind of a breeze does our presence represent? No doubt all of us have experienced ourselves as an icy blast on others or maybe a scorching heat. If we are honest, we have had to acknowledge the effects of that, that perhaps something was prevented from happening that might otherwise have happened.

Personal atmosphere is the largest component of an individual's expression. We tend to think of our mental output or our physical abilities as our particular hallmarks, and yet a person's quality of atmosphere is where the real hallmark is. That is where primal changes take place, and the sphere from which the most profound influence can occur. There is a way of letting this influence from

ourselves begin to be clearer, to be more consistently a warm breeze.

There is a power in ourselves that we haven't realized. Perhaps we haven't seen how important our own attitudes are, nor how possible it is to let them change. If we acknowledge responsibility for the effects that our attitudes have on others, then it is increasingly easy to allow those attitudes to change, soften.

A little passage from the writings of Lao-tzu speaks about water:

> The softest of stuff in the world
> penetrates quickly the hardest.
> Insubstantial, it enters where no room is.
> By this, I know the benefit
> of something done by quiet being.
> In all the world, but few can know
> accomplishment apart from work,
> instruction when no words are used.

I think the softest stuff in the world is true innocence of atmosphere, in which our own being and the being of others can have their accomplishment. There can be accomplishment without trying to manipulate anything. Where we have tried very hard to make things work we know that they have become more and more tangled, more difficult, and we feel ourselves more frustrated, because we were trying to get in where no room existed. But there is a special and unique quality within us, if our windows are open, that *will* penetrate. It is only the softest of stuff that will go in where apparently "no room is," where maybe the attitudes of others have been hard or judgmental toward us. Can we not let our thoughts and actions flow from that core place where we are innocent, where we know ourselves as strong and beautiful without all the layering of stuff by which we tend to define ourselves and each other?

We are used to defining ourselves by our characteristics and limitations. "I've always done it this way. This is the way I am." Though familiar, these definitions in fact fit us uncomfortably. For instance, perhaps I feel that I'm not organized enough, and that I should be more organized. So somebody says, "You can't depend on her; she's so disorganized." Then feelings of defensiveness, shame and anger rise up, triggered by the comment. But I, in essence, am neither organized nor disorganized. I simply am. Knowing this, I can look at the way I operate and be soft. "Yes, maybe I should have done it another way. Maybe I can learn from this person. Even if what was said seemed harsh and unfair, perhaps there is something in it that I can receive and think about—a kernel of truth that I can accept and use. I, in my invulnerable center, may be objective. I can remain open to whatever should come next and see how things change."

A symbol in our own bodies of this process of change is breathing. The lungs are one of the primary organs of purification for the body. The heart pumps the blood to the lungs, where the toxins that may be present in the blood are absorbed into the lungs and are expelled with the carbon dioxide. Then oxygen is available to nourish the blood as it moves on. The process is of movement, change, continual purification.

The word "repentance" has tended to have a heavy connotation. For most people it implies

grief and shame and hanging onto what happened. Thoughts about what we feel ashamed of
often go on and on until we think we've paid
enough for it, whatever it was we did. But I
think there is a simpler, more efficient experience
of what could be called repentance—not trauma-
tic, just a momentary release.

In the same way our bodies easily let go of
impurities in the breathing process, emotional
and mental toxins can also be released in a natural way. When a feeling arises, for instance,
that I experience as a toxin—maybe I feel resentment about something that happened, and I know
resentment is unwholesome—rather than holding
onto it, I can consciously use my breath and exhale it. The resentment isn't really me; it's part of
something surrounding my self; it's "out there."
So I just let it go, exhale it.

We have impurities going through our
bloodstream all the time, and if we hang onto
them we contaminate ourselves. But there is no
need to develop toxic conditions if we see ourselves as a living, breathing clearing house for
whatever comes through our minds and our feelings. Let the breathing take care of it. Let oxygen,
pure air, whatever we know to be pure, be taken
in. And when we breathe out, we can let go of
whatever is in feeling or thought that isn't
lifegiving.

I've observed that no matter how much good
intention somebody may have about peace in the

world, until that person has a certain degree of
purity of atmosphere, the toxicity having decreas-
ed, he or she cannot experience peace. Our responsibility is to take care of our own toxins. As
individuals, we must take care of our own breathing process, our own letting go. Depending on the
clarity of what we experience internally, peace
can be present—in ourselves, in our households,
and in the world.

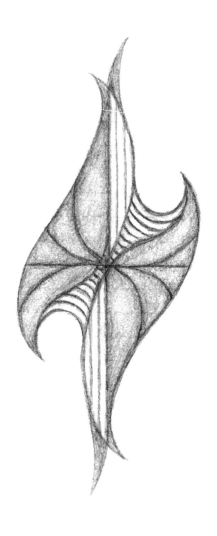

*What we really long for in communication
is communion, the transcendent interaction
where we deeply understand, and are understood.*

6.

Communication and Communion

M any people feel an excitement about new discoveries in technology—improvements in our ability to move around and communicate across the world in various ways. This impressive technology tends to reinforce the hope that science and cleverness will solve all our problems. But has technological prowess enabled us to reach each other more meaningfully? With all of our communicating, what is it that is being communicated?

Our hopefulness about impressive communication systems may arise out of the fact that we have all experienced the pain of miscommunication in our more immediate, daily situations.

Regardless of the means we use to reach each other, what carries fundamental importance is this question of human contact, and the potential emergence of what could be called communion.

There isn't one of us, I'm sure, who hasn't felt at some point that we wanted to say something to someone and we didn't know how to say it. We may have felt a sense of deference, or perhaps we were afraid of the consequences in some way. There is so much pressure on us not to make waves, and at times our perceptions may even include so much that we're not really sure what would be the right thing to say, so we tend to hold back and not say anything.

On one hand we find barriers in expressing ourselves, and on the other, in our ability to hear and receive. So much of our communication is actually listening, and we need to ask ourselves how developed our ability is to hear each other. We have all known the experience of being angry at someone and therefore not really hearing what they were saying, or being prejudiced about a person's appearance or manner of self-presentation and just blanking out what it was they were seeking to convey.

Our emotions play a huge part in our ability to listen. Perhaps we could think of emotion as a substance. There is a space in each of us which is filled with one kind of substance or another, and this emotional substance is either permeable or impermeable to communication. Depending on what we are "filled with," we are able to receive and hear, or we are not. I'm sure we could all name some impermeable emotional states, such as anger and prejudice. Hurt is another. When there are hurt feelings you just cannot hear what someone is trying to say; it's all blocked out.

What can fill our internal space so that we do hear each other? What is it that will provide contact, rather than these separations to which we are so accustomed? What feelings are permeable?

Pondering this, I began writing a list of various emotional states. My first thought was that love, for instance, would be permeable, and anger would be impermeable; but then I realized it is not as simple as that. We tend to use one word to label a whole variety of possible experiences. For instance, there is both an impermeable and a permeable state of love. Though we would assume that love is one of the primary feelings that connects us, allows us to hear each other, there are types of love that aren't permeable. They say "love is blind." Infatuation, being fastened on someone, blots out all the rest of the world, and the voice of reason falls on deaf ears. But there is another kind of love which is open, simply allowing both individuals to be, and to change, and to grow, knowing that a nourishing bond of mutual acknowledgment and joy is always there.

Another quality is caring, which we usually think of as connecting one person with another.

But caring can be very exclusive, such as when a mother is overly concerned for her children and can't let others develop a friendship with them or provide elements that would help them mature. That kind of caring is quite impermeable and produces imbalances, whereas another kind of caring is secure and understanding, providing a base from which the child may freely develop many avenues of potential.

We could consider assurance. We may feel assured because we think we have things all

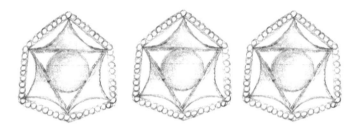

figured out, but that's extremely impermeable. When someone is aggressively pursuing a goal and is sure that they "have it made," there is no way of getting through to them. But when we are assured that things always work out, one way or another, especially if we stay relaxed about them, then that form of assurance is permeable and allows us to maintain connection with each other and stay in balance.

There is both an impermeable and a permeable state of humility. It may not be an emotion, but is an attitude, a way of feeling. When some-one feels they are "no good," that kind of humility is quite impermeable. They are not go-ing to hear, they are not going to be able to com-municate. We all have felt "no good" in one way or another, and this feeling has blocked off what could have been shared. But there is another type of humility where we simply say, "I don't know what should happen" or "I can't judge how that person should be." That opens us, and allows the connection.

The whole experience of communication is in-ternal. We have a great range of choice in what feelings we entertain, or give space to. Maybe we don't realize how much choice we have. We think we "get along with so-and-so" and we "just can't communicate" with someone else. But our own state, whatever fills the internal spaces in ourselves, is our individual prerogative. We can choose in any moment to let go of what clutters—anything from a flicker of judgment about someone, to an impulse from a deeply-rooted past imprint. It's our choice in the moment to retain it or let it go.

What we really long for in communication is communion, the transcendent interaction where we deeply understand and are understood. Well-being and communion are available, but we tend to trample the seeds of understanding between us with all of our trying and opinions and uncertainties.

As we begin to watch our step and respect the possibilities in our simple interchanges, we may be surprised at who appears in our lives with whom this understanding, this communion, may grow. Here is the sweetness of fulfilment coming unbidden. We can't, successfully, arrange our lives according to our preferences, deciding whom we wish to be close to. When we withdraw our criticisms and self-determinations, new potentials open up unexpectedly and our lives fill out in ways we never could have planned.

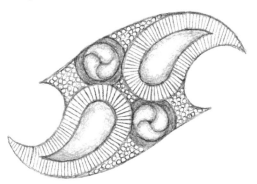

Here is magic. A larger pattern of relatedness begins to appear, a pattern that is useful to the purposes of life itself. As we let ourselves be permeable to what is being said by the people and situations around us, we find that something larger, even universal, is being said. It is actually this voice to which we are giving ear, and though we perhaps can't explain it we know that in our listening and our speaking we are coordinating with that universal Word.

Women Together

Rhythms of shared effort,
doing,
regardless

        The curve of lip,
        a secret sparkle eye to eye
        across the room

    A penetrating word
    that raises pulse and issue

        Within a womb of listening
        tears melting old
        hard places

The drenching sweetness
of embrace
amidst a shower of peony petals

As we dare to relinquish expectations,
the richness of the universal currents may fill our lives,
the flow of the yin and yang,
the enjoyment of the creative pulse.

7.

Yin and Yang

The magical flow of currents between the masculine and feminine principles is natural to us, but our understanding and experience of how these principles work is often unclear. If we see where we have inadvertently dammed up this flow, we can begin to let these currents move freely in a complementary way.

In a televised "Citizens' Summit" between the U.S.S.R. and the U.S., Vladimir Posner, who was moderating from the Soviet side, quoted the famous line from *My Fair Lady*, "Why can't a woman be more like a man?" He observed that this attitude is more pervasive than we might think, and tends to characterize even international relations: "Why can't the Soviet Union be more like the U.S.?" and vice versa.

The male/female principle is basic and vital to our whole life experience. Perhaps because it is so elemental to our makeup, our beliefs about male and female have become the most ingrained, and often mistaken. Our grandparents at least, if not our parents, were prone to judgments which we ourselves have absorbed. Few mothers have not said, "Isn't that just like a man?" And maybe we can remember our fathers or grandfathers saying something like, "Oh, don't tell her. She'll just make a big fuss and ruin everything." These stereotypes were the beliefs of those times. People really felt they understood how the male and female operated.

Presently our views are quite different, and other sets of beliefs are supposed to be more accurate. However, no belief system can offer the true pattern for an individual. Trying *not* to act out the old stereotypes, because of prevailing fashion, has produced its own kind of artificiality. For example, the new assumptions about how male and female should be, have sometimes engendered fear of forthrightness in men, and hardheartedness in women, preventing an organic blend of individuals.

Genuine openness is the beginning of discovery. Elemental male and female principles are at work within each of us, in every aspect of our lives. As we relax we can explore the authen-

tic dynamic between masculine and feminine—
their essence within ourselves, in relationship to
others, and between groups and nations.

The Oriental symbol for yin and yang il-
lustrates this relatedness of male and female. The
picture is of a circle, divided evenly into dark and
light by an S-curve, with a light dot inside the
dark, and a dark dot inside the light portion. The
yin (feminine) and the yang (masculine) are por-
trayed as of equal importance, each needing the
other to produce balance, wholeness, and each
having some of the other's nature as part of
themselves. The male and female principles are
interlocked in their function. Throughout our
lives we sometimes embody the yin to another
person's yang; at other times it is we who embody the yang.

The masculine and feminine principles appear
in many forms, easy or uneasy, in our family

relatedness. The dynamics within a nuclear family have the potential for either chronic frustration and sadness, or profound fulfilment and delight. We have all observed the tangle of uncertainties and misassumptions with which most people emerge from childhood. Observing the effect of those on an individual's way of relating to yin and yang elements in the world at large, we can see how important it is that the family unit be honored as a crucible for individual learning and development. Here is an arena within which one may learn to function creatively in either the yang or the yin role, because one's true self transcends any role that is played.

The delicate rhythms and pulsations among the members of a family unit are usually hidden in everyday exchanges—the way we say yes or no to a suggestion, the way ideas are allowed to combine, the safety of consistent tenderness, the willingness to listen and take time. In my own family setting I am conscious of the yin quality that I often contribute to my husband's yang way

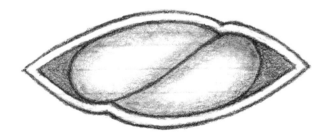

of thinking. There are also times when the directional yang is more mine, and I am very grateful for the yin of his quietness and receptivity. This interplay is not only observed but is also felt by our two children.

We have a teenage son. As a parent, I am the yang in that relationship and he is the "feminine" yin to me. This is an important phase in his life where those positionings must become diaphanous, transparent, so although I still have ultimate authority he can begin to feel his yang effect on his world. He needs to find his own differentiated identity and to begin to see what is produced by his actions and words.

In the next ring beyond our families, these dynamics are no less intensely experienced. In organizations and businesses, for instance, many people play both roles. The employer is yang to the employees' yin, but those employees have their own responsibilities and might be yang to others who work under them.

Predictable modes of thinking and feeling tend to arise in those who consistently play one or the other of these roles. Those in the yang position usually feel that though things may not be quite perfect they're really going along all right, whereas the sensations of being in the yin position often include, "But I haven't been heard. If only they would listen, if only my input was accepted, then things would be much better, because I can see all kinds of things that are wrong." People tend to take on the identity of their roles, fastening these attitudes on themselves as people, and become complaining employees or hard-hearted bosses. If we acknowledge that our jobs are simply roles we are playing, temporary roles at that, then we can relax and let ourselves, our authentic selves, be above whatever role is being played. We can begin to understand each other from another vantage point.

On the international scene we can look at someone like the President of the United States in an essentially yang position. The President has massive armaments and recognized economic power behind him, and his attitude tends to be, "Things may not be perfect but overall they are under control." In contrast we may look at the Soviet side in their relating to the U.S. There is the feeling that they are not being heard and that there is no basis for trust, no basis on which to work things out, because from their standpoint the American attitude has been insensitive and hard-hearted. We see in marriages that go on the rocks that the man, at the point of agreement to divorce, is often quite bewildered, saying, "It wasn't perfect but I thought everything was basically okay." And the woman says, "But I tried to tell you! I've been trying to tell you for years. I just can't stand it any longer!"

In all interrelatedness we need to understand what the dynamics are from the other side of the fence. If we can let ourselves be above this

male/female dynamic and understand why the existing attitudes are present, we are much further along in understanding how to let true peace be established.

In either role the internal work that is needed has to do with expectation and judgment. We come with a set of expectations that is more or less automatic, and when another person does not fulfil our expectations we tend to feel resentment and anger, perhaps even fear. What is at fault? Is it really the other person, or is it our expectations? Can we not suspend our beliefs that other people should operate in a certain way? As we dare to relinquish these expectations, the richness of the universal currents may fill our lives, the flow of the yin and yang, the enjoyment of the creative pulse.

When we play the yang role, the ability to trust our own instincts is crucial to our field of responsibility. What is most necessary to us is our integrity. It is only as we scrupulously maintain our integrity that we can trust ourselves. If we don't, if we deny what we know is right—rationalize away the right thing to do and follow self-centered compulsions—we become scrambled. We don't know what to trust.

For those who play the yin role, the demand to be heard needs to be tempered with the acknowledgment that one *will* be heard as one is worthy to be heard. As we are more reliable and responsible, there is a base of substance from which we can operate. We realize that it's not really the squeaky wheel that gets the grease. It may seem so temporarily, but in the long run that approach generates no love, no respect. The worthy person eventually is heard—the person who has been willing to see the larger picture, to be consistent, and to give without demands.

Each of us has the whole world for our context, a whole world into which to give. Every relationship, every situation, is a perfect setting through which we can observe our self-expression and learn the nuances and rhythms through which our unique selves can be given.

As we maintain a clear sense of self, regardless of what role we are playing, then any role can be played well, skillfully, accurately, and the design and flow of the universe can be manifested through us in creative and delightful interaction.

If we acknowledge that our relationships are not
for our own fulfilment, we discover
that our togetherness has a larger value and purpose.

8.

Men and Women

The masculine essence and the feminine essence are very different from each other, and men and women often see things from opposite vantage points. In our everyday world we also find differences in social conditionings which, if we don't understand them, tend to separate men and women from each other. Boys and girls often grow up thinking quite differently. It can be very helpful for us now, as adults, to consciously understand these differing thought patterns. When each begins to understand what it is that has "made the other tick," we see how much error there has been in the way we have been approaching each other.

In an article entitled "Why can't he hear what I'm saying?" Deborah Tannen has defined some of the differences in the way boys and girls grow up. Habits tend to be established in thought and communication because of the patterns of relating that boys form together and the patterns that girls form together. Out of those experiences come the automatic assumptions that men and women use as the basis for their communications with each other. These assumptions inevitably give rise to disappointment and anxiety, because what is meant and what is heard are often two different things. Here are some excerpts:

Little girls tend to play in small groups or, even more common, in pairs. Their social life usually centers around a best friend, and friendships are made, maintained and broken by talk, especially secrets. The secrets themselves may or may not be important but the fact of telling them is all-important. It's hard for newcomers to get into these tight groups but anyone who is admitted is treated as an equal. Girls like to play cooperatively. If they can't cooperate, the group breaks up.

Little boys tend to play in larger groups, often outdoors, and they spend more time doing than talking. It's easy for boys to get into a group, but once in they must jockey for status. One of the ways they do so is through talk, telling stories and jokes, arguing about who is best at what, challenging and sidetracking the talk of other boys, and withstanding the others' challenges in order to maintain their own story and consequently their status.

When these boys and girls grow up into men and women they keep the divergent attitudes and habits they learned as children, which they don't recognize as such but simply take for granted as the way people talk. Women want their partners to be a new and improved version of a best friend. This gives them a soft spot for men who tell them secrets. As Jack Nicholson once advised a guy in a movie, "Tell her about your troubled childhood. That always gets them!" Men, on the other hand, expect to do things together and don't feel anything is missing if they don't have heart-to-heart talks all the time. If they do have heart-to-hearts, the meaning of those talks may be opposite for men and women.

To many women the relationship is working as long as they can talk things out. To many men the relationship isn't working out if they have to keep talking it over. If she keeps trying to get talks going to save the relationship and he keeps trying to avoid them because he sees them as weakening it, then each one's efforts to preserve the relationship appear to the other as reckless endangerment.

It's a revelation to begin to understand each other's way of thinking!

Misunderstandings and lack of perspective are responsible for so much pain in relationship. Many elements of assumption contribute to the impasse that partners sometimes reach in a marriage. One typical scenario develops when a woman loves her husband but feels that he has bungled things so often that she can't trust him. So she starts to very subtly maneuver, and watch, and be critical. When the signs appear that he is going to do it again, whatever it is, she gets tense and tries to prevent the replay: "Oh God, please don't let it happen again." She gets her claws into him because she is afraid: something is going to go wrong, something is going to be damaged. That is her side of the experience.

The husband's side is that he has other things to think about. He may have all sorts of responsibilities that he is trying to take care of. The marriage was pleasurable to begin with, but as this standoff develops he begins to experience his wife as a burden rather than as an enjoyable companion. He is always being poked at and tugged from the side, and he doesn't know how to handle it. He is uneasy about the fact that he can't count on her, afraid of what influence she might have. He also feels ashamed of his own mistakes, his weaknesses, his dependence on her.

Underneath the woman's apparently competent exterior she is ashamed of being so critical, demanding, manipulative. She knows it isn't healthy, but she is afraid and can't seem to help it. With this combination of fear on both parts and shame on both parts, a locked and seemingly hopeless situation develops. Each partner has been wounded and has reason to mistrust the

other. We have a world in which everybody apparently has reason to mistrust everyone else. What is it that can begin to cut through this tangle?

The beginning point must be stillness. Just coming to a point where we are quiet and at rest in ourselves makes an immense difference to our perspective. Honesty is another requirement, because we can't get anywhere without each of us acknowledging what we have done to create whatever difficulties have been present. Facing the facts of our own behavior opens the door into a new experience. We may re-examine our priorities and motives and realize that what has seemed so important and has been driving us is not worth the sacrifice of what we most deeply value. Honesty and a sense of proportion are inseparable.

This is such a complex world. Even the smallest situation is very complex, and no one person can say, "Yes, I know exactly what should happen here." We eventually have to let go to some kind of larger ecology—a gut-level sensing that all is well and that the right direction will emerge if we continue to be honest and genuinely give of ourselves. Nothing works until we finally see that the most important thing to care for is the spirit emanating from ourselves. It really doesn't matter who said what stupid thing, or who looks how desirable. The point is: What am I expressing? Is it actually something true? Is it a helpful influence? Am I willing to simply listen, willing to let things work organically, without trying to get in and force something to happen? As that attitude begins to be taken, it's amazing how our experience of one another is magically transformed.

But transcending the differences, whether it has to do with male and female as such, or differences in personality and conditioning, isn't an end in itself. It's not something that we must get together and pursue, just so that we'll like each other more or so that we'll feel better about ourselves. If we acknowledge that our relationships are not for our own fulfilment, we discover that our togetherness has a larger value and use. Agreement in spirit, regardless of what needs to be worked out in the "nitty gritties," is the simple requirement for that discovery. Two people living together with a sense of purpose and agreement, day by day, generate between them a potent atmosphere that is much more than the simple addition of two single individuals. This atmosphere is the medium through which magic can work, a part of the overall design by which we may take care of our greater responsibilities.

In our pas de deux,
broad-based and gentle,
 you step, toned and focused,
 I, free and fertile,
in confluence of stride and turn,
 rippling through the days.

9.

Relationship

When two people find a balance
together, maintaining a bond of honesty
and agreement in spirit, the creativity of one is
also part of the other. Fulfilment is multiplied,
because each has his or her own field of responsibility and expression, but also shares in the
generation and productivity of the other. This
book, for example, is an expression of myself as
a woman but is not separate from my husband
Michael, and I have felt his enfoldment
throughout its creation.

Michael and I are very different, and since
our marriage in 1967 we have gradually learned
how our differing viewpoints and natures can be

complementary. This chapter on relationship contains our combined substance, and it seems natural to include some of his thoughts along with my own.

There is an unquenchable yearning in the human soul for right relatedness with others. An endless number of books are written and pored over, and movies explore every permutation of what we call love. Psychiatrists attempt to assist in the sorting out of past relationships so that present ones can clarify. In our own lives, what foundation may we find that will allow us to simplify our experience in this complex realm and discover what is inwardly true?

What we really long for in relationship is that all the parts of our lives fit together. Much of our time and energy is devoted to a few close connections—parent, child, friend, spouse—but we actually exist in a tapestry of relatedness with all people. Our natural experience is of communion not only with a special few but within a whole pattern, and our balance within that is our fulfilment.

Whether in a committee meeting, in a crowded airport, or in a bedroom, we have a specific kind of relatedness to whoever is present; there is a right way of being together. To let a true pattern form, we must be able to perceive the right proximity between ourselves and others. A business acquaintance, or a friend we telephone once in a long while, may be fairly distant. Someone else might be naturally closer and it is right to be together more frequently, or more intimate physically. The perceptions of these right proximities are available to us, but we tend to override them by letting our established compulsions and desires govern us. False hungers arise because of the voids in our sense of self, and we attempt to fill them with other people. But as our experience fills out from within, those wants and hungers fade and we begin to have the space for finer perception. We can then receive the signals, which have been there all the time, as to what is true. There is in fact no fulfilment if, for example, we are trying to get someone into a closer proximity than is valid. In the end we must acquiesce to that internal signal, and let things move and be as they will, so that a design of potential inter-relatedness is allowed to fill out.

What is authentic self-expression, which then connects genuinely with other people? We can't be accurate and creative in just one or two relationships. We are either right in ourselves or we aren't. If we are expressing ourselves accurately, then our relatedness with anybody, at whatever distance, has an authenticity to it that is satisfying and creative. Michael's view includes a world awareness in this regard:

> It has seemed over the centuries that the most secure relationships have been between people who are blood-related. Even though there has been

animosity within blood families, there nonetheless has been some security in the maintenance of this family identity with its boundaries and traditions. But we are in an era now where something else is beginning to emerge. The traditions of the past are breaking down by reason of our present life-styles, and we have the opportunity of seeing that everyone is connected. Things are very different now from what they were a hundred years ago, when there were smaller pockets of people located around the world. Now there are more than five billion of us and the planet is turning into a "global cottage." We are all in this house, and we are all related. It begins to dawn on us that there is an inherent order to things, and that we all are contained within one overall relationship. We all interrelate, and it is a matter of discovering *how*.

I would wager that in large cities most of the hundreds of thousands of people experience a tremendous sense of isolation and separation, maybe buffered a bit when special events come along. Then people get stirred up and begin to feel that they have some kind of civic pride, something which gives them a sense of belonging. But the day after, they wonder where it went. In actual fact, all people are family. It is a strange image to us, because there is such a pervasive sense of isolation. But we are all on earth together, and I suspect that where there is a greater openness to respect the integrity and purposefulness of the whole, we will find a depth of relationship with far more people than we ever imagined. This takes place when we are not expecting anything from anyone but we simply have the space within ourselves to receive others, and to let them be who they are and how they are. Can we truly be intimate together in the deepest, most meaningful sense?

In the more personal and intense levels of relatedness, virtually everyone experiences what could be called shadows—frustrations and fears and shames. Now that there is so much more awareness of psychological elements, almost everyone has analyzed him- or herself to some degree: "I feel fear or desire in relationship to that person because my father didn't do this or my mother did do that." The tangle inside may be acknowledged, but what to do about it? We have to face the fact of these shadows and the futility of our usual ways of trying to deal with them.

There has been so much conversation about what we require from a relationship. ''What do I need? What do you need?'' Sometimes something can be accomplished through this kind of interchange, but our awareness must expand to include another level of being, the very essence of ourselves. We can't be authentic just at the emotional and mental levels, because we have dimensions above that.

There is what could be called our spiritual nature, where our deepest sense of purpose resides. Often around puberty there is a rush of this sense of purpose. Think back to childhood or the early teens; perhaps you remember an experience of sensing your own greatness and meaning in the overall design of things. Without this sense of personal destiny being touched again, I don't think we can find a way to deeply relate to each other, because we are actually part of a larger design, a grand rhythm at work.

We can easily see the rhythm of spring following winter, or the sun coming up every morning. Unconsciously relying on this, we already do know our place in this larger scheme of things to some degree. This rhythm works on the grand scale, but it also works in detail. In the natural world every plant propagates according to its own nature and thrives within the balance of an overall ecology. Is there not the same potential for us in a way that we haven't yet discovered?

Michael is very aware of the natural world and what it represents in human experience:

One of the reasons why people feel so isolated from each other, why they have such difficulty in interrelating, is because of a fundamental sense of separation from the way life actually works. Humanity's relationship with the earth and its systems has largely been lost. There are those who have been taking steps to reawaken their awareness of the inherent order and design within the natural world. If the world of nature is not respected, various complications ensue. This is why, for example, there is a major farm crisis right now in North America.

Over the last number of decades we have pro-ceeded very deliberately with our technology, us-ing increasing amounts of chemicals—there are 45,000 agricultural chemicals currently on the market—and we have run roughshod over the natural systems of the earth. The end result is a barrenness in the environment as a whole. Because there has been this loss of respect for the natural order of things, the environment of the planet is in grave danger of total collapse.

It is not a matter of everyone returning to the land and hugging trees—although there is nothing amiss with going into the wilderness; I think we can often benefit from that—but of really recogniz-ing that there is an innate order of things that we have lost track of somewhere. There needs to be space in our hearts to listen for that, to take it into account, to let it be primary. Then all the other things in our lives will tend to sort out in relationship to that, including our connections with others.

How do we open a space for this deeper sense of ourselves and our place, and therefore the intrinsic pattern of our relatedness? A critical step in this discovery is letting go of wanting, of desire. This may seem a rather revolutionary thing to say, considering how relationships are handled currently, because there is the assumption that "unless I want, and unless I state my wants clearly, I won't have." That really isn't true. If we want, we isolate ourselves. We actually block the very process of receiving, because any degree of obsession closes off the natural flow, and the true pattern of our overall experience can't appear. When we open a space by letting go of our desires, both giving and receiving are liberated, and we are an integral part of the universal flow. There is a rich kaleidoscope of relatedness that can emerge, constantly changing and constantly beautiful, but we have no idea of what that could be as long as these shadows of intent and desire are cluttering up our inner space. We may let go of the shadows by acknowledging, "I don't need to want in order to have."

For my own part, I have discovered that no want is legitimate. If one accepts that as a basic truth, the shadows that have been present begin to dissipate, because one is in a stance of responsible expression. If we care for what radiates out-

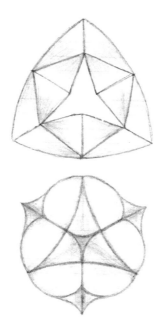

ward rather than being so concerned about what is coming *to* us, that radiance creates a field through which whatever we genuinely need can come to us.

There is so much fantasy surrounding comforts and desires—the fondling of little memories or the resentment about what didn't happen. We let ourselves off the hook in our imaginations. A common monologue is, "I deserve this indulgence because I'm under such stress, or because I don't have what I really need. I work hard. I do so much that nobody notices. This won't hurt anything. I deserve it." As we come to accept things as they *are*, in simplicity of heart, this monologue is transformed into: "I don't have to

demand anything. I am simply and fully myself.
I have what I need as I act honorably and loving-
ly in this moment now." And though it takes
stepping from one internal place into another—
and it may take some time to learn to stay
there—we find that that statement is true.
Michael has this to say:

> Perhaps a synonym for "wanting" could be "ex-
> pectation," which covers some of the same ground
> but also emphasizes preassessment of how things
> are and where people are at. The fact that we tend
> to rely heavily on our pre-judgment produces all
> kinds of unnecessary confusion.
>
> There is a story about a Prussian foreign minister
> in the nineteenth century who, when he heard
> that the Russian ambassador had died, said, "I
> wonder why he did that!" We tend to have built
> into our makeup—certainly at the diplomatic
> level—all kinds of suspicions, which are brought
> forward from generation to generation and may
> have no more validity than that absurd conjecture.
> Yet we are convinced in the moment that they do.
>
> It is crucial to see beyond the external form of
> things to a deeper reality. We tend to get hung up
> on the immediate details of life and what another
> person's habits may be. While the immediate issue
> may need attention, there can be something else in
> our own awareness of the situation, of that person,
> which recognizes him or her as an important part
> of the picture. We can't really do this beyond the
> point of the experience of our own worth. Prob-
> lems arise when we have uncertainties concerning

ourselves, and the problems are resolved when we express the best of ourselves. It's all linked together. If we are deliberate in our acknowledgment of the reality in others, that very expression from us reinforces our own sense of self.

Trust is one of the major issues between people: "How much can I trust you?" "Can I trust you to still love me in twenty years?" "Can I trust you to behave so that I feel safe with you?" Because everyone is growing and no one is complete, there are what could be called untrustworthy elements that appear, and people wound each other without wishing to. But what is it that we can trust? Again, it is the fact that we are actually contained in an overall creative process. *That* is trustworthy. Because each one of us in these closer relationships is contained in the overall process, and we trust that, then we ourselves aren't so vulnerable. We don't say, "I have to trust you to be safe," because if I feel myself in that larger process, then I *am* safe. I can give you the space to grow as you need to and I can grow as I need to. I implicitly trust the fact that the process will continue to work.

There is a law intrinsic to Universal Process: nobody gets away with anything. We can be sure of that. If we are honest we know that we reap the seeds we sow, and that other people must reap the seeds they sow. We don't have to make sure people "get what they deserve." How do we know, in any case, what anyone else deserves? We can mind our own business, confident that the process is inexorably at work.

This has many implications for handling emotions. Jealousy, for instance, is the absence of trust. It could be described as the fear of loss. Because interrelating has so often been on the false basis of trying to fill internal voids, both in oneself and in the other, relationships have been fragile. A wife instinctively knows that if someone comes along who fills her husband's voids more attractively than she does, his attention and energy will swing away from her and what had been built between them will disintegrate. Even in small situations this subconscious fear can arise as jealousy. But if we are not feeding off each other, because we are individually whole and secure within the larger context, we have a foundation for working out the situations that come up.

It is only when we are secure in singularity that we can successfully operate in plural, that we can offer true complementation to one another. Then jealousy disappears, and we realize that each of us has room for an infinite number of people in our heart, with no two occupying the same space or providing the same complements. It is no loss to me, for instance, that many people have a place in Michael's heart. I have learned that I can relax with the many connections we both have with others. What is important is that the current of love between him and me be free and true, that our communication be deep and complete. There is momentary balance in that, and no worry about present or future.

Michael's perspective on the matter of trust is simple:

So often the attitude is: "Can I trust you?" But maybe the question really should be: "Am I trustworthy?" We seldom seem to ask that. If there is an increasing sense of one's own placement within the larger context then there can be some steadiness in oneself, and that is the beginning of trustworthiness.

Because this steadiness hasn't been generally experienced, people try to sustain their relationships
by hoping to please each other, but that never really works. It's like the cartoon in which one man
was commiserating with another. He said, "I
became more sensitive to her needs, learned to
understand her more, and I even learned to cry.
Now she says I'm a wimp." While a woman may
feel initially that she wants a man to hear her, in
fact if that's all he does, if he doesn't have any inner strength of his own, the relationship will end
up being very unsatisfactory. Though he has at-
tempted to somehow fill the woman's needs, there
is remaining discontent. In and of itself it may
seem generous and considerate, but without his
having a sense of self as a man, what he does ends
up weak. And that isn't satisfying to either
partner.

Many of us have come together in our immediate relationships on the basis of fantasy. We
had beliefs perhaps about the security that would
be obtained by entering this relationship, or the
fulfilment of romantic views of one sort or
another. Those things, generally speaking, are
discovered after a while to be illusory, and at that
point there is often a threat of breakdown. We
must come to a deeper reason for being together.
Once we begin to sweep aside this initial and
rather childish reaction, we sometimes find that
there was something else happening of which we
had no conscious awareness at the time. There was
a reason contained in the larger context. If we stay
put long enough to let the dust settle we'll begin to
see what that is. But there is a very definite period

for most people of appropriate disillusionment, which then may open the door to what is truly authentic.

Because partnering has often happened on the basis of illusion, when the disillusionment comes, part of working responsibly with the process may be to acknowledge that it is more accurate for the two people to be related in some other way than a marriage. Almost invariably people marry images. When the images are dispelled, if one can face the present situation responsibly, regardless of what has gone before, there are always things to be learned, areas to be clarified. It is an opportunity for personal growth and for enlarging one's vision. Sometimes that means acknowledging that there is still a reason to be close, and sometimes it is acknowledging that a different proximity or positioning is right and true. If we listen carefully to the inner signals we learn that we can be content with whatever is being indicated. We may begin to rest in the fact that those signals are in tune with much more than we can consciously grasp.

What brings a sense of meaning in the combining of people is the creation of something together. That's why children are sometimes given so much focus within a marriage, because the two people have created this together and are responsible together. But there are many other levels of birth and creativity that are natural when lives are synchronized. Harmony and the experience of being in sync come because we focus on something besides each other. We give our attention to what is to be accomplished; then we flow together.

Michael sees all relationship as relating to purpose. Why relate? Why are we together?

If it is just to satisfy something in ourselves, it will be a pretty small and limited experience. It would seem that there has to be a larger reason for our being together. I think we need to ask that question relative to sexuality. Why sex? Is it just so that something can be fulfilled in ourselves, or so we can gratify the other person? Or is there a larger reason for it all? If a person has no sense of greater purpose in sexuality, the experience may be initially interesting and different when it's new, but before long the edges are worn off and he or she is left with Dullsville! There is something so vast here to be known. I don't think one can label and describe what that is, but the knowledge of being contained within a larger picture makes all the difference.

Whatever stance we take internally shows itself in the world round about. What we are doing to the environment as a whole is not very pleasant and is essentially a reflection of the way we view ourselves. We look out and see, for instance, that the earth's rain forests, one of the sources of our oxygen, are being destroyed at an amazing rate and will be gone by early in the next century. We see this urgent problem, and there is the inclination to rush out to do something about it in an external way—God knows what, actually, because the problem is so huge and complex. And this is repeated in many different aspects of the world's environmental situation.

But there is something much more immediate to be addressed, which has to do with one's own authenticity of expression. Abuse of one's own earth, one's own body, is reflected outward into the environment. When you have millions of people doing that, then you have disastrous repercussions. The resolution comes not by desperately trying to wipe the reflection off the mirror but by changing the place where the reflection originates, which is in our own selves. We have a contribution to make to the big picture by the way in which we handle our own lives.

We are very good at rationalizing the fulfilment of our wants. "There must be something divine about this. I received a message from God that this should occur. We are obviously meant for each other!" But the questions should always be asked: Does this fit? Does this really work? Is there something that is useful here in the larger context? These questions are rarely considered.

The real answer is contained in the word "passion." Where is our passion? Is it possible to let a passion for what is true, for what carries the note of integrity, remain primary always? That's what is needed. A burning core current must be discovered within ourselves; it isn't extracted from outside somewhere. It's something that is already within us and finally has to burn out into the open. That's what the world is crying out for.

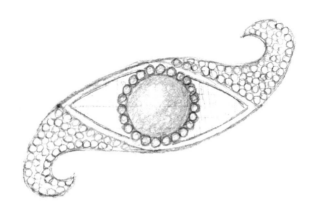

There are so many tender and vulnerable aspects to our world and to our own natures which cry out for understanding and wise care. Unless a passion for the truth is motivating our lives, we will inevitably violate and destroy. Most of us have experienced a sense of having been violated. This is certainly a large part of the message of the women's movement, which has acknowledged that there has been violation and has encouraged women to stand up and say, ''I am uniquely myself, and my experience mat-ters.'' At the core of all the anger discharged through these decades is the sense that there is something sacred that has not been acknowledg-ed. As women have come to value themselves, new dimensions of internal growth have been possible. In more recent times the realization has begun to dawn in the hearts of many women that if their own selfhood is sacred, then the selfhood of men must be sacred too.

Recognizing the sacred core of all things is the basis for a range of connection rarely known between people, because this sense of the sacred is not exclusive. If I recognize it in my own being, and in the being of one other person, I experience that connection as part of the sacred earth, a part of the cycles of growth and change that go on all around me. Our deepest yearning is for this sense of belonging to one sacred whole.

This obviously relates to sex and to physical intimacy. As Michael has said about the earth and her natural resources, the automatic tendency of human beings has been to say, "This is here for me, and I will do what I can with it to make my life better." That's virtually the same attitude that is common in regard to sexual experience: "This is for my pleasure, my fulfilment, and I'll get what I can." It often ends up in misery because the sense of the deepest self, the sacred self, isn't present. Only when we come back to that sacred place in our beings, that awareness of ourselves as pure and meaningful, can we perceive what is appropriate in intimacy and sexual expression, and experience our bodies as beautiful and worthy.

In many people there is an urge toward variety in sexual experience—different partners, different positions, different techniques. But the physical world is as it is; it can only contain a narrow range of options, and by themselves they don't really satisfy. When we stop demanding the physical dimension—the body—to give something it can't, and instead begin to see sexual experience as an expression of sacredness, of one's participation in the greatness of universal design, we make a new discovery: the variety is really with the invisible factors, which are completely different every time two people are together. Here is freedom, letting the physical way of being together clothe appropriately the invisible essences that are our responsibility to bring forth. In this spirit of offering, of listening for what is true for that moment, we find we can give ourselves in a way that was not possible before. And this opens the gates of passion, the flow of natural variety, and the contentment of having let a holy and beautiful current come into the world.

All that is in this world is within our care, and every word we speak, every act we undertake, can be a reflection of our love for the sacred. As any given moment is acknowledged as sacred, we cannot in that moment allow something to fill mind or heart that is not consonant with that stance; it must be relinquished. In that letting go, moment by moment, all shadows are dissolved, and new dimensions of our own value and beauty are unveiled.

Communion

Currents
in the air of
our conjoining inner landscapes
let the voice of spirit
speak
in whispering leaves
or rushing wind
to which the meadow grasses
love to bow.

Sacred gifts of Self in Other,
Word
and wordless Voice
beneath the sky

The world situation must be freed
to realign along natural lines of force,
which we can participate in but cannot determine.

10.

What Can Be Done?

This planet we live on is sacred. It is becoming obvious to many people how we as a race have desecrated the earth. Everywhere we look major crises are appearing, and the problems seem insurmountable. Our usual response to an urgent situation is to get busy and try to fix it, either out of fear or out of a sincere desire to help. But this avalanche of global difficulties can stimulate us into unnecessary and ill-considered action. Using the same approach that created the problem in the first place, we can't fix it, whether it's the educational system, the environmental crisis, or the arms race.

We have to finally face the fact that in our attempts to counteract the things that aren't right, we just complicate matters more. We have to come to the point where we acknowledge that ultimately we don't even know what the progression of change should be to bring balance into the world. Individually, or through legislation or well-intentioned projects, we can't fix it, we can't unscramble the eggs.

Something entirely new is required, starting with an acceptance of the state that is present now. A change of heart, not a change of ideas, opens the way to an all-encompassing answer. Only the Universal Magic can heal, can allow new vitality and order to emerge. The world situation must be freed to realign along natural lines of force, which we may participate in but cannot determine.

This earth is our home and so the problems belong to all of us. How will we put our house in order? We may sense that all of these things need to come into balance—that there needs to be reforestation, that the damage to the ozone layer must be halted, that the world economic system must be brought under control, that nations should be able to work together. But the imbalances have actually been created by our attempts to *make* something happen, by our good ideas. Sincere people have made innovations, "breakthroughs," found more sophisticated methods of doing this or that, but the catch isn't seen until much later.

Who had the foresight to know that the Western nations' well-meaning aid to Africa would do more harm than good? Africa is strewn with the remains of failed development projects. It was arrogantly assumed that Western approaches should be transplanted into this completely different setting, and the result has been a shock to the African social and ecological system. Millions of dollars of capital have been poured into supposed help, and yet there has been decline in the local standards of living, and the number of tons of food required from outside sources has doubled in recent years.

On the North American continent, who could have predicted that the scientific breakthroughs of the last forty years would have produced great tracts of exhausted land in the American Midwest? The hybrid grains and corn that would grow quickly and produce greater profit, perhaps even feed the starving Third World, required heavy chemical fertilization and then proved to be so weak that massive application of pesticides and herbicides was necessary for their survival. This vicious circle—increasing economic outlay for more chemicals, and the soil itself being more and more depleted—continues to escalate; and what is left is dust.

One after another, the good intentions have gone awry. World problems have never been solved on this basis. It may be almost too much to face, but at some point we must acknowledge that though there seem to have been brilliant answers to some of the problems, each answer has in fact created more problems. Essentially the world is in the worst mess ever.

Everywhere in nature we can see the fact of inherent design. The intricacy of the ecological tapestry, or the minute perfection of detail in the most complex of organisms, demonstrates that there is an innate intelligence in every level of life-form. In seeking to offer something constructive through our lives, it would seem the best part of intelligence to learn how to integrate with the design that unifies this great life-form of our planet. There are clues all around us as to how this interrelatedness works, symbols even in our own bodies.

An exquisite example of design and power in the human body is the system of endocrine glands. Although it has been studied extensively, this system still contains many mysteries. Throughout all of the changes we experience and the challenges we meet during the course of our lives, we unquestioningly trust this crucial system to do its job. These small glands are the masters of our bodies and are responsible for the overall regulation of the thousands of processes that go on in this amazing physical mechanism we live in. If there is the slightest imbalance in one of these little endocrine glands, our whole life experience is affected, becomes unbalanced.

The hormones secreted by the endocrine

system have a regulatory effect on the complete range of human function, from thought and feeling to reproduction and digestion. These essences are more concentrated than we can imagine. A fairly well-known hormone, for instance, is adrenalin, which is secreted by the adrenal glands and assists in handling the stresses and demands of everyday living. In a crisis situation a surge of adrenalin can produce a tremendous release of energy. There are many stories of people who have performed astounding feats of strength such as lifting a car off a trapped child. And yet all the adrenalin these tiny glands produce over a lifetime amounts to only about a teaspoon. That's concentrated power!

This system can be seen as a metaphor for what could happen in the body of humankind as a whole. Is it possible that those people who take a new stance of focus and purpose in their lives could have as potent an effect as the endocrine glands, symbolically, in the whole body of humanity? Just as the hormonal releases from these various glands are subtle and minute, a similar concentrated power resides in individuals and is available for release.

It is an interesting fact that the cells of an endocrine gland secrete internally; in other words each cell secretes individually, and its essence is released directly into the bloodstream. If we use this as a metaphor for our function as individuals, we can see that our "secretion," that which emanates from us, has a direct effect on the whole "body" of humanity. Since our contribution is released directly into the "bloodstream," which is the conscious and subconscious flow of human experience at large, we don't need overt means of communication to affect each other.

We tend to give so much weight to the power of the media, for instance, and it is assumed that a person who gets onto TV or is published has a particularly strong influence. Over the ages, however, there have been individuals of great stature whose emanation has been very potent on a different basis altogether. Their lives were based on momentary integrity, practicality, and awareness of purpose. They didn't have mass media to broadcast their thoughts at the time, but their influence and authority were vast, even affecting the course of human history.

There is something here for us to observe about the potential in one individual. Regardless of the beliefs and traditions of the times they lived in, these remarkable people relied on the effectiveness of the simple experience and expression of what was true in the moment. Is it not also possible for us to remain stable and true, unmoved by the impulses from all the conditioning factors of our time? It is a rare person who will trust his or her own integrity regardless of how a circumstance seems to be going. Such people are like cells in an endocrine gland, providing a balancing, regulatory "secretion." Who will provide this essence, this impulse, carrying a message of wholeness?

Those individuals who remain true-hearted and open to whatever may be accurate and real in their lives, not wanting their own way, not being afraid of what is unfamiliar, are the ones who can provide a healing, stabilizing factor in the whole human body. Such people are, in truth, making themselves available to be employed by the universal regulatory processes.

Something new is pressing to come forth in human experience, and if we don't accommodate it there is every indication that we as a race will destroy ourselves, one way or another. We must learn to move with Life's impulses.

Accommodating this new current, we find there is a design and control working through us without our mental understanding of all that is involved. As we simply remain in place, the magic of our inherent power is at work, and is part of the force moving all things toward resolution and active balance.

Peace is a function of being part
  of a vibrant and purposeful whole.

11.

Peace

In such a turbulent world we all long for peace. For my own part, I find I don't think about world peace very often, because I am assured that peace is a natural side effect. It is a result of other factors coming into balance and is not something that can be produced because we wish it or envision it or try to arrange it. Peace in a household or peace between nations is an effect of what happens at another level, an invisible level of cause.

The absence of peace is based in fear and shame. Because we have all carried these factors, the resulting antagonism and defensiveness in us as individuals have ultimately produced the same stance in nations. In addressing our own part in the global situation we must ask ourselves, "Why am I afraid? What is it that I am protecting?" Honest consideration of these hidden motivations is crucial to the emergence of world peace.

As a race, we have a set of centuries-old habits. We assume that we will not be of value unless we "make something of ourselves." We think we need to structure our lives so that they will contain at least a modicum of fulfilment,

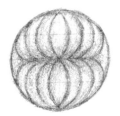 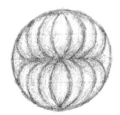 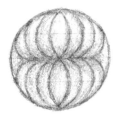

looking for "the right partner," "the right job," "the right location," etc. And because we seem to be thwarted in these attempts to make our lives work, we assume that the universe is hostile.

Changing our premise is the first step to changing our conclusions about the world we live in. There is a symbol which seems a very apt representation of what is happening in the world: cymatics, the field of study which explores the effect of sound on matter. A given substance, such as sand or glycerine or oil, is placed on a membrane. Then a given tone or note is sounded, which visibly activates that substance. The most remarkable patterns appear—beautiful mandalas; echoes of forms in nature such as a cross section of the stem of a plant; a dance of droplets bursting upwards. Different musical tones produce different patterns, and likewise each type of substance responds in its own way.

It is obvious in this symbol that the substance must be malleable and responsive for a pattern to appear. Here is where we must question the premise of our lives and consider other possibilities. Perhaps, symbolically, we have held the substance of our lives rigid, unresonating, because we have assumed we have to produce the structure for ourselves. Our opinions and desires, our accusations, our regrets about the past, all lock our substance into unmoving "blocks."

I wonder if the current of life itself, that which powers the universe and organizes the natural world in such impressive ways, is not akin to a tone sounding. I wonder if, for us, something as simple and internal as an acknowledgment of that Tone would not begin to let our substance be released into a larger pattern that could form. It seems obvious that conflict arises because individuals and nations have historically tried to create their own patterns, even if they have had some altruistic hope that the patterns might fit together reasonably.

But humanity *is* one. There is a grand ecology into which we naturally fit, and conflict will not cease until we relax and allow ourselves to be put together by the Tone of life. Peace is a function of being part of a vibrant and purposeful whole.

Each individual is unique. Each part of the world also has its unique character and qualities. I think a fear can arise that if we let go of our views and intentions we will be swallowed up, be nullified. But if we look at the natural world, the variety of what is present is no less than stunning. It seems to me there is a safety we have barely touched, the safety of yielding into a larger pattern—a human ecology, we could call it— which contains inbuilt checks and balances. Because we have been so self-determined and unaware, we have little experience of what it would mean to release ourselves in this way. Yet we trust nothing more implicitly than gravity, for instance, which keeps the earth at the right distance from the sun and plays a part in the orderliness and function of all the life-forms we know.

As we release the substance of our lives by learning to suspend judgment and by giving up our trying and defending, we find that a new and meaningful pattern begins to appear. This pattern can automatically include everyone on earth, showing itself especially through those who are flexible and resonant. Here is the genesis of harmony, a peace more complete than any of us may have dared to hope for.

The less one tries,
  the more one actually achieves.

12.

The Grand Rhythm

Often in guided meditations, in order to evoke a sense of oneness, a sense of large proportion, we begin by focusing on the physical place where we are. Then we imagine our perspective rising, so that we look down on the building; then rising higher, we are able to see the whole city. We move up until all the surrounding land is in view, and still higher until we can see the earth at a distance and even see the working of the solar system and how everything swings together so perfectly. That grand view could make us feel small, but it doesn't really, because the viewpoint from which we can see

our doings on earth in perspective is in fact
natural to us.

There is a general tendency to become
enmeshed in the small daily things—the struggles
to achieve, or the fears, the pleasures, the hopes,
the goals—experiencing them as so large that they
blot out our view of the greater picture. And yet
we have an instinctive sense that we as individuals are important, that our presence actually has an effect all around this globe. Immersed
in the small goings-on around us, we feel we
have to try very hard, and we inflict pain on
ourselves with our trying. Even a sense of responsibility can spur us to trying. Yet what I have
found is that often the less one tries, the more
one actually achieves.

Freeing our consciousness to move upwards,
we begin to feel the presence of a Grand Rhythm.
There is unimaginable precision of design in the
way galaxies move through each other without
collision. We may acknowledge the wonder of intrinsic rhythm in all of this, but we generally
haven't noted that this rhythm comes through
ourselves as well. We have tended to assume,
"That's all working fine out there, but in
something more immediate I have to manage it
myself."

I would wager that the unproductive behavior
we observe in ourselves and each other arises
from this very mistrust, the fear that we can't let
go to this larger rhythm. All of the punishment

that we inflict on ourselves and impose on others
is not the way to effect change. Unproductive
behavior only begins to be relinquished when
one realizes, "I don't *have* to do that anymore, I
don't have to be harsh and aggressive," or
whatever it is. A feeling of safety begins to come,
safety in the universal order, and suddenly the
whole view is changed: "I don't have to do
that." And one can relax.

A friend of mine has for years been struggling
with a sense of insecurity. She has had emotional

tugs-of-war with her husband, not approving of his behavior half the time and yet being terrified that he wouldn't love her anymore, being jealous of his having even a two-minute conversation with another woman. She realized that all of this was very unproductive and yet was not able to change it.

At a certain juncture she spent some time apart from her family to just relax, let go, and begin to experience these deeper rhythms that are part of the very earth from which we spring. She wrote these words in a letter, and has agreed to their use here:

"I find it so extraordinary, the feeling of dichotomies blending: that the more alone one allows oneself to be and feel, the more one is absolutely meshed into oneness. The more space one creates in a relationship, the closer one becomes. The less one is involved in apparent issues, the faster and more easily they dissolve. The less one fears, the safer one becomes."

What a beautiful articulation. Often we don't realize how bound we are and how possible it is to just take the step to relax and be still. It can open a flow from deeper resources, making the way for profound transformations in experience.

We may wonder sometimes where inspiration comes from, or unexplainable easing of tensions, or resolutions appearing in what seemed insurmountable difficulties. We can't observe our subconscious realms, but they play a huge part in our life experience.

At the turn of the century one of the greatest mathematicians of the time was Jules Poincaré. A genius in the field of theoretical mathematics, he had remarkable insight into the workings of the subconscious. In exploring new mathematical relationships he would unexpectedly come upon beautiful patterns of elegance and harmony. He made this observation about inspiration: "The sudden illumination is a manifest sign of long, unconscious, prior work."

We have a wonderful capacity in our unconscious, our subconscious realm. It is the realm of magic, the realm from which something beautiful and new can suddenly break surface. We have been quite afraid of our subconscious and its workings. Certainly that subterranean part of ourselves has contained a mixture of elements, creative and destructive. We all have experience of the trouble we have caused when an ungoverned compulsion has arisen, we have followed it out, and some kind of damage has ensued. Feelings of shame, as well as a sense of responsibility, have prompted us to keep the lid on our urges, but in doing this we have also put a lid on the magic that could unfold through us.

Even if we haven't consciously acknowledged it, we wish for the innocence, the cleanness, in the subconscious realm that would allow our impulses to flow in a free and creative way. But how to get from here to there? A beginning point is acknowledging that we are meaningful parts of a sacred whole. "The less one fears, the safer one becomes." We must be genuinely willing to let anything go that is not a true part of us, to allow any thought or behavior to come into the cool light of morning. If we keep anything hidden by wanting our own way, we maintain those shadows in our subconscious and we will never be able to trust the clarity of our impulses. The more we can relinquish our attempts at managing the world, the more space magic has to work through us.

The "long, unconscious, prior work" of this cleansing process centers on Truth. Holding simply and consistently to a truthful tone in going about daily affairs, we may unexpectedly find that shifts have taken place in realms we cannot reach consciously: vision clears, love is present, an elegant resolution to a question suddenly appears.

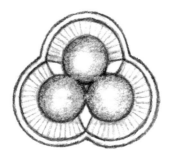

Perspective is crucial in this ongoing clarification, because the stirrings from the subconscious are often felt so vividly, so acutely. I enjoy this little poem on perspective:

And so, if the rain falls today,
will the sun nevermore be seen?
Unlikely.
And if, in sudden fury,
the snow bundles a spring day,
is warmth forever lost?
I doubt it.
Or, should the ground look brown and barren,
do we cry for lack of seed therein?
Of course not.
A tiny wheel within a tiny wheel within a tiny
    wheel.
Why then the furrowed brow at circumstance
of strange motion?
Rest in the sunlight.
Abide in the Wheel above the seasons,
gently amused and most kind.

(Beth McCarthy-Dice)

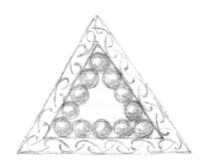

As we keep our perspective, both from the standpoint of the view from above and the trust of the perfect workings of what is below, we find our experience growing in breadth in both directions. We can allow things to be experienced in all their acuteness—the snowstorm or the apparently dry ground—because we know that the larger rhythm contains everything, and change is continual. We can abide in trust, even if the immediate situation looks difficult or painful. We can remain "gently amused and most kind," and the effect of our presence on earth begins to be kind and creative at all levels. The unconscious work which is ours to do continues, and then in a moment of magic we may note its emergence into awareness.

But what is not visible, what is happening underneath, has an ongoing effect as well. It is not just what we think consciously, what has surfaced, that has an effect beyond us; it is the whole spectrum of our being. The responsibility for this whole spectrum is indeed an easy one as we trust the Grand Rhythm around us and the echo of that rhythm in our very blood.

Artesian

Underground,
the gush of water:
hidden deeps of distant longing,
caves where power
waits and surges,
running ceaseless,
silent splash.

In surface browns and greens,
a waiting:
roots of trees
yearn downwards, reaching;
finding rock,
no silent splash,
content themselves with rain.

Running ceaseless,
waiting, hidden,
waiting for the slightest earthshift. . .

Now the cleaving open,
surging,
letting move the rock and gravel,
open, yes,
sweet water coming,
truthful gush, the springs of being,
springs of joy,
artesian
singing,
purifying surge of water,
upwards,
up,
at last comes coursing
into light
and air.

Our experience of the Grail is only possible
when all that we are and all that we have is released,
allowing it to move in an upward flow.

13.

Whom Does the Grail Serve?

The meaning of the quest for the Holy Grail is elemental to us as human beings, and the story appears, in different clothing, in cultures all around the world. The twelfth-century European version, by Chrétien de Troyes, is the earliest known written account of the search by Parsifal for the chalice, the Grail, used by Christ at the Last Supper. The story contains interesting metaphors for the spiritual process. Two characters that embody valuable symbolism for us are the wounded Fisher King, who is the guardian of the chalice within the Grail Castle; and Parsifal, the innocent fool.

In the story, the Fisher King has been wounded early in his adolescence. This occurred when he came upon an empty camp in a forest and tasted a bit of a salmon he found roasting on a fire there, causing both severe burns and an awakening of the sense, through the taste of the fish, of what was possible to him. This wound, which also is described as a wound in the thighs, keeps him from being productive. It will not heal. So he spends his life in agony, and it is prophesied that only when a wholly innocent fool arrives in his court will the healing be possible. The Fisher King's wound affects not only himself but his whole kingdom. The land is unproductive and desolate, with sorrow everywhere.

The youth Parsifal, who doesn't know his name until much later in the story, is raised in a remote and insignificant place. He grows up completely untutored and simple. One day he happens to see five splendid knights, by whom he is dazzled and inspired, and sets out to King Arthur's court to become a knight himself. He is indeed knighted by King Arthur but is still completely without skill or training. He is taken in and tutored by Gournamond, a godfather figure, in his castle. Besides all of the necessary training for knighthood, Gournamond instructs Parsifal in two important matters: firstly, he is never to seduce or be seduced by a woman; secondly, when he reaches the Grail Castle he is to ask the question, ''Whom does the Grail serve?''

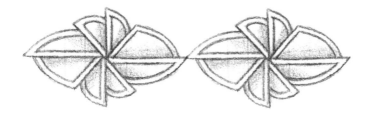

After various adventures Parsifal comes to the Grail Castle without realizing what it is. He is received ceremoniously and partakes of a great banquet. The Grail is passed to each guest and produces whatever food and drink is silently wished for. Parsifal, overwhelmed by the magnificence and the magic that is present, fails to ask the necessary question, "Whom does the Grail serve?" In the morning the whole court has disappeared, and once he has left the Castle it too vanishes, leaving him with an insatiable hunger to have that perfect experience again.

In Parsifal's journeyings from this point he subdues so many knights, sending them to Arthur's court, that King Arthur searches him out to properly honor his stature and accomplishments. But during the celebration in King Arthur's castle, a hideous damsel appears on a decrepit mule and recites a list of his sins, the primary one being that he had been in the Grail Castle and had failed to ask the right question. Parsifal was responsi-

ble for the fact that the Fisher King's land had re-
mained barren and in mourning. She says he
must go and find the Grail Castle again, and this
time must play his part.

Parsifal experiences many years of search,
becoming hardened and bitter, but then is unexpectedly brought back to his original vision and
innocence by an encounter with a hermit. Ab-
solved of his past, he needs only to ask for the
Grail Castle with all his heart, and he finds it
immediately.

The de Troyes version of the story stops here,
but others go on to describe the completion of the
cycle in various ways. The important element is
that Parsifal have the courage to ask, "Whom
does the Grail serve?" The answer is: "The Grail
serves the Grail King." (The Grail King, represent-
ing deity on earth, has lived always in the central
room of the Grail Castle, in constant communion
with the Grail.) With this realization comes the
release of the Fisher King's torment, he is healed,

and the land can once again flourish and its inhabitants experience joy.

Robert Johnson, in his perceptive and penetrating development of this myth in the book *He*, points out the relatedness of these and other characters to processes and aspects within each individual. Although his approach focuses on the application to men and their inner workings, it is relevant also to elements in a woman's nature. There is something universal to be seen through this story.

Whatever our state of physical, mental and emotional health, there are levels at which all of us have been wounded. The Fisher King wound in us has produced barrenness and grief somewhere in our lives. As in the story, simply being near the Grail is of no help to us. The Fisher King could not touch the Grail because of his wound, could not be sustained or healed by it. The abundance available because of the Grail, the possibility of happiness all around one, cannot be received until the wound is healed.

Parsifal, whose name means "innocent fool," represents the humility and innocence we must allow into our internal "court" before this release can happen. As in the story, this experience of innocence often comes from an unexpected place, just as Parsifal was raised in a remote and unnoticed part of the kingdom.

We all have experienced the grief of knowing that happiness was available to us but that for some reason we couldn't reach it or receive it. When we are in this state, the very fact of our inner turmoil makes it impossible to be part of the flow of abundance that we can see in nature and in certain people around us. The human tendency is to lament the wound, to struggle for healing; but healing comes when the Parsifal aspect of our nature, that which is humble and simple, is allowed a place internally.

The initial instruction never to seduce or be seduced by a woman is a key to Parsifal's final achievement of the Grail. The Grail represents the Holy of Holies, the highest and most pure of feminine quality, which in union with the Grail King represents perfect and ecstatic happiness. If one is seduced by one's inner woman, by the feelings and desires that appear, the purified state of peace is never possible. We may find we have stumbled into the Grail Castle in moments of transcendence and joy, but if the proper question is not asked the experience disappears, leaving a greater ache and hunger behind.

It is the human habit to assume that whatever is present, from inner feelings to outer commodities, is there for our own benefit. Given this assumption, we are never in control of our lives but are being seduced one way or another constantly by our fears and desires. It seems there is no way to happiness, to the possibility of even nearing the Grail, without this constant struggle to obtain and defend.

But the innocent must take courage in hand and ask the question, "Whom does the Grail serve?" The answer that changes everything is that the Grail serves the Grail King. The experience of purity is only possible when all that we are and all that we have is released, allowing it to move in this upward flow. This requires not only courage but honesty.

Whom do our own bodies serve? If there is healing needed, if there is suffering, what is its meaning? If our bodies and minds rightly serve the purposes of the universal order, and not our own limited wants and ideas, that acknowledgment is a profound release. We can then be patient with their cycles, because we are not seduced, demanding anything of them. The objectivity that has seemed so elusive now becomes possible: we care for our minds and bodies on behalf of the Grail King, to whose service we are pledged.

Although in the symbolic story this question need only be asked and answered once, we find in our internal journeyings that it must be asked again and again. Just when we feel we have accomplished something, are figuratively in King Arthur's court, receiving acknowledgment for something well done, the hideous damsel always appears to remind us that we are not yet whole, there is yet more to do, and we must set out again. We must face her, acknowledge our faults and omissions, and carry on.

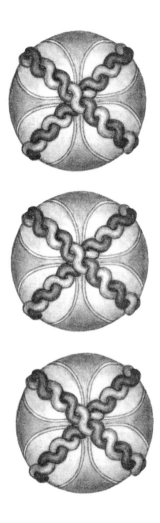

If we lose our Parsifal innocence we may waste years in frustration and blame of others, hungering for what we dimly remember is possible. It is ironic that what years of effort can never achieve, humility and sweetness will achieve immediately. Parsifal accepted the absolution of the hermit, and in that moment released all the hardness and regrets of his past. In this release is the magic of a clean heart, which then finds itself resonant with the majesty of the Grail Castle. And one can be admitted easily.

All who are within the Grail Castle are aware of the meaning of the Grail, the purpose of all the abundance of the earth and the pleasures and possibilities therein. As it is acknowledged, deeply, that the Grail serves the Grail King, that this abundance flows both from him and to him, our wound of isolation and barrenness is healed. We become part of the grand order and we find new delights and peacefulness appearing in our lives.

The Grail represents the purified experience of the feminine aspect of ourselves. It is said that "virtue is its own reward," but in this sense virtue also allows us to truly experience the pleasure of the rewards that come to us. When we give up trying to make or get happiness it inexplicably appears.

It is another paradox that in fighting for individuality we only maintain the pain of wounding, whereas releasing ourselves into humility, even if we appear foolish or insignificant, allows the right question to dawn on us. As we acknowledge that we, and everything, rightly serve the Grail King, that grand and universal process within which we are in fact contained, that apparent giving up of individuality is the healing of our wound. We find, like the Fisher King, that our own domains begin to flourish and prosper, and our own kingship can be administered uniquely. Individuality, we realize, is a function of playing a significant part in the larger whole.

The Fisher King wound is evident in all of humanity—in the grief of alienation, in the fact that health difficulties are rampant regardless of medical advances, and in the abuse and exploitation of the natural world. Healing on every level is available, but someone must ask the necessary question and let the answer penetrate.

Purification

No wants, no wants.
Let the Fire burn!
This incandescent aching
is a question of my soul.
Hold true, true,
while the flames lick all around,
consuming what they will;
I remain.
What may be burned away
must go, must go!
is ultimately dross, and ash.
O yield, yield,
be tender in the Fire
as what is right and beautiful
unfolds.
No wants, no wants.
I am safe, complete,
and in this perfect
stillness
allow myself on wings of
angels
to be borne into the
   cool
   blue
   center
of the Flame.

In the Beginning
is the Word.

We as individuals carry power
and are part of a larger pattern
in which power moves through earth and tides,
seasons and thoughts and words.

14.

The Return of Magic

Amid the familiar doings of our lives, our responsibilities and daily interactions, there are moments when a different dimension is sensed, and we may marvel at the inexorable way a resolution has come, or catch our breath at a beauty we cannot describe. The word "magic" has become hackneyed by advertising, trivialized by overuse, and we might shrink from naming these precious, secret moments in that way. And yet what better word do we have with which to name and understand the less visible aspects of our experience? For surely we as individuals carry power and are part of a larger pattern in which power moves through earth and tides, seasons and thoughts and words.

Perhaps out of fear we have denied our own power, knowing that sometimes it has surged out of control, caused tragic damage. We have set things in motion which we did not intend; then all we could do was sit helplessly by and watch the cycle run its course. But we also know the power of being in the right place at the right time, the penetration of providing the crucial element by which a situation clarifies or comes to fruition. We have felt the triumph of facing some personal devil or unproductive habit and finding it dissolve before our eyes.

Perhaps we could describe two levels of experience: High Magic and Old Magic. What can be called the High Magic relates to conscious awareness: the development of skill and knowledge, seeing the reason for things. We also have in our very blood what could be called the Old Magic: intuition, lusty earthiness, awareness of times and seasons, a compulsion to growth and to the honoring of cycles. We may think of ourselves as dominant in one aspect or the other, but we are not whole without both. In the realm of the High Magic, it matters what it is we know or have not yet learned, and how we define things to ourselves. In the realm of the Old Magic, what matters is *who* we are, where and with whom we are, when we come and go—that each of us is unique and there are things for

which one is responsible which cannot be touched by any amount of power through anyone else;
they are one's own to do.

Our culture has become so linear and cerebral
that "reason" has been made an idol. Yet it is not
through reason that even the High Magic always
works, but through openness of mind, allowing

admission to factors which linear reason may
crowd out. And certainly reason does not remote-
ly touch the realms of Old Magic. One cannot
reason even oneself out of sadness, let alone
understand why a collective sadness exists. Those
resolutions are in the realm of the Old Magic—
that which cannot be manipulated, which works
inexorably, according to its own nature. There
are elements in our subconscious which cannot
be clarified except as we begin to let the Old
Magic work truly.

The realm of myth, of archetypal images, can give us some useful vocabulary for observing and sensing the elements at work in us, and for learning how to function wisely in relationship to them. In many myths, for instance, what appears innocent for a time can house the most insidious of evils. In our own experience, how can we know? How do we perceive what is really the case in any situation? Our own compulsions and perceptions have been such a mixture we may well wonder what to trust. But the truth in the observer is always the basis for discerning the truth of a circumstance. We do have a touchstone internally: what is the truth of myself, my larger purpose, my place in the whole? In this context we may sense accurately what lies behind the visible in the events around us.

Many ancient and mythical stories describe a sacred horn which is to be blown only in the worst extremity of danger, and help will come. The note from that horn can symbolize something very important for us. The sound from the horn is what brings change. It seems to have no direct relatedness to the conflict going on around, and yet that pure sound evokes something new.

In our own lives we may see conflicts, even an extremity of danger or destructiveness. There is a note within ourselves which we must learn to listen for, a tone that carries sweetness, truth, assurance. As we sound this tone—the note from the ancient horn—in our thoughts and words, something new and clear begins to appear in our experience.

In many whom I know, there has been an increasing experience of unfamiliar stirrings in the heart, of feelings arising with unexpected vividness, of situations that had seemed settled suddenly being in flux again. Our reason tends to be dismayed at this—it is so untidy!—and we have no way of knowing in what direction things will move next. It is now that our ability to accommodate the Old Magic must awaken. We must first learn how to hear and then to sound the note of Truth from the sacred horn. Its sounding sets up a resonance within which the Old Magic can move to a true resolution.

When things get hot, both in our own lives and in these symbolic portrayals, the automatic tendency is to be engulfed by fears and try to save or right the situation somehow. The High Magic is necessary here: the skill to know that the direction of our attention is crucial. We give attention to what is creatively possible, letting our energies move into that. Fearing the evil feeds the evil. The archetypal wizard, representative of the High Magic, rightly does not go out and become embroiled in battle. He would endanger himself and therefore the larger responsibilities he carries. His place is in his sanctuary, aware of what is occurring, assisting as he can, but letting things work as they will. This wizard-consciousness is rightly part of our own ability to comprehend and encompass the changing scenarios around us.

In most stories of magic there is recognition of the potency of words. In the form of incantations they can kill or cure, make or unmake. Words are perhaps our most obvious tool of daily magic, though we have tended to ignore their potency. We have demanded the right to say what we think, describe what we observe, regardless of the cost. Since the realm of words is fully open to us, it would seem the course of wisdom to begin to wield them consciously. If we are intelligent, if we are apt students of the High Magic, we will note what we have created and shaped by our words. We will let our utterances be purified and refined, so that there is no evil in them.

The true impulse through both the High and the Old Magic is to create, to bless, to clarify. This pervading impulse, which arises from our deepest selves and is the essence of the universe around us, could be called White Magic. It is this pervading force that operates the continuum of Old and High in our natures. This life-impulse is perfect, and the continuum of Old and High is perfect, but distortions in our experience have appeared because of our resistances and self-determination. Our first responsibility is to let go, to let our feelings and our awareness clarify because our concern is to provide cleanly what is ours to provide.

As that sense of purpose becomes more distinct and the darkness is dispelled in our own experience, the power we carry is more and more evident. Our responsibility is a large one: we are at a juncture when the world's future is hanging in the balance. It is indeed a time for White Magic, the enfolding light of love and the penetrating tone of truth. This grand Magic, by its very nature, carries the seeds of fulfilment and of ultimate strength.

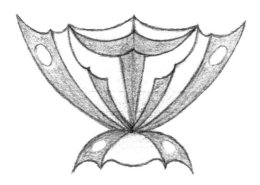

Artwork

The drawings in this book were done over a period of some twenty years. Each one begins simply with a sense of number, such as a two or a five, and when that number of points is placed on the page, the space around and between them gradually fills in. They were drawn freehand, and were to the best of my ability an expression of the invisible design present in each time and place.

Nancy Rose Exeter

About the Author

Nancy Rose Exeter is an accomplished lecturer, counsellor and seminar leader, as well as a loving wife and mother of two teenagers. She spends several months of the year travelling worldwide on speaking engagements with her husband Michael, and together they share the responsibility of coordinating the international Emissary program.

Born in 1946, Nancy Rose was raised in Colorado in an intentional community established by her parents, Lloyd and Kathleen Meeker, and now lives in a sister community in central British Columbia, Canada. The B.C. community, established in 1948, is home for some 130 residents and is affiliated with similar centers around the globe.

From 1981 the author and her husband carried the British titles Lord and Lady Burghley. In 1988, with the death of Michael's father, they became the Marquess and Marchioness of Exeter, giving Michael a seat in Britain's House of Lords.

Over the years Nancy Rose Exeter has come to be known not only as a friend but as a trustworthy point of spiritual orientation for many women throughout the world. In addition to her wide range of correspondence, she maintains a passionate interest in the fields of drama, dance, musical composition and poetry.

Under the names Michael and Nancy Burghley, she and her husband co-authored *The Rising Tide of Change*, featuring excerpts from their public presentations.